About Pets

the Labrador Retriever

A guide to selection, care, nutrition, upbringing, training, health, breeding sports and play

about pets

Contents

Foreword

The book you are holding is a basic 'owners' manual' for everyone owning a Labrador Retriever and also for those who are considering buying a Labrador Retriever. What we have done in this book is to give the information to help the (future) owner of a Labrador Retriever look after his or her pet responsibly. Too many people still buy a pet before really understanding what they're about to get into.

This book goes into the broad history of the Labrador Retriever, the breed standard and some pros and cons of buying a Labrador Retriever. You will also find essential information on feeding, initial training and an introduction to reproduction. Finally we give attention to (day-to-day) care, health and some breed-specific ailments.

Based on this information, you can buy a Labrador Retriever, having thought it through carefully, and keep it as a pet in a responsible manner. Our advice, though, is not just to leave it to this small book. A properly brought-up and well-trained dog is more than just a dog. Invest a little extra in a puppy training course or an obedience course. There are also excellent books available that go deeper into certain aspects than is possible here.

About Pets

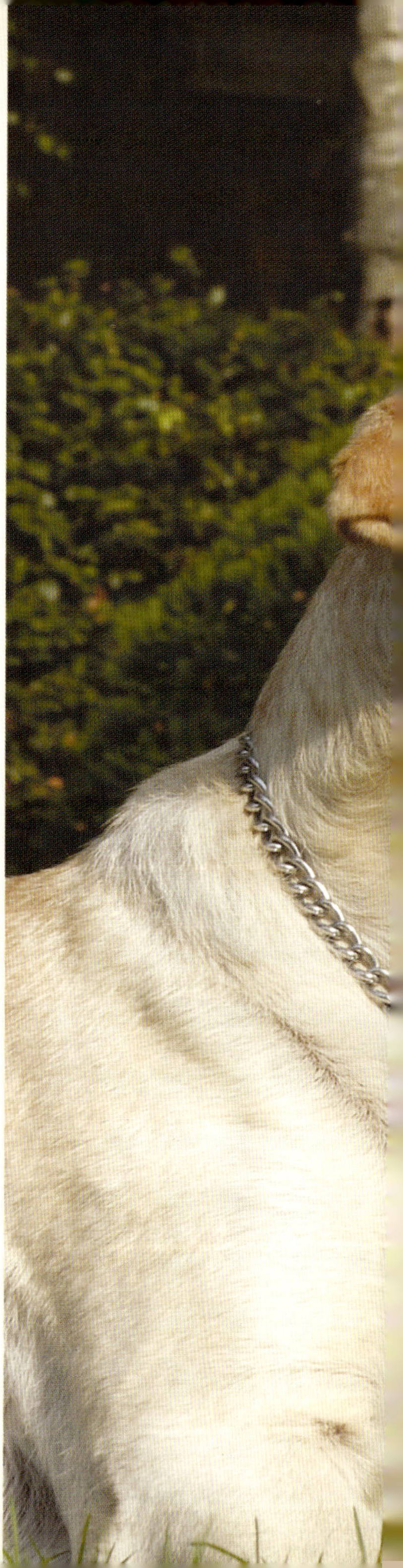

about pets

A Publication of About Pets.

co-publisher United Kingdom
Kingdom Books
PO9 5TL, England

ISBN 1852791942
First printing
September 2003
Second printing April 2005
Second printing April 2005
Third printing Februari 2006 - Revised

Original title: de Labrador retriever

About Pets,
Warffum, the Netherlands
www.aboutpets.info

Photos:
Rob Dekker, Rob Doolaard, Henk van Welzen and Helga Barrau

Printed in China

In general

The Labrador Retriever is one of the most popular dog breeds in the country. It owes its popularity to its friendly nature, its good behaviour with children and an unstoppable urge to please its master.

This last attribute makes it particularly useful as a hunting dog; indeed there's no dog that retrieves better than a Labrador Retriever. In fact, the name says everything. To retrieve means to fetch something and bring it back. A Labrador doesn't only do that in the country, but in other places too. It is often used as a tracker dog to search for illegal drugs. It also serves well as a guide dog for the blind.

Origins

Despite its name, the Labrador Retriever actually originates from Newfoundland (Eastern Canada). The confusion in the name probably results from the fact that the island of Labrador is close by. At the beginning of the nineteenth century, two new (black) varieties of the Newfoundland Dog appeared. The larger variety became known as the Newfoundland and the smaller as the Labrador or St. John's Dog.

English fishermen fishing off the coast of Newfoundland took the smaller dogs with them to England. They were especially popular with nobility as a hunting dog. The dogs were also crossed with Pointers, Setters and other Retriever varieties.

In 1903, the Labrador was officially recognised by the English Kennel Club. The club also registered Labradors that were born from cross-breeding, which often led to disputes at shows. A group of dissatisfied owners then started the English Labrador Retriever Club in 1916, after which the registration policy was changed.

UK Kennel Club and their breed standards

What does the UK Kennel Club?

In their own words: "The Kennel Club is committed to developing and supporting a nation of responsible dog owners. As well as organising events and campaigns to help dog owners meet their responsibilities, the Kennel Club also produces a range of literature to assist the dog owning public."

What is the use of a Breed Standard?

The Kennel clubs answer: "The basis of breed shows is the judging of dogs against the 'Breed Standard', which is the prescribed blueprint of the particular breed of dog. For all licensed breed shows, the Kennel Club Breed Standards must be used for the judging of dogs."
More about the UK Kennel Club Breed Standards: "The Breed Standards are owned by the Kennel Club, and all changes are subject to approval by the Kennel Club General Committee. New Breed Standards, for newly recognised breeds, are drawn up once the breed has become sufficiently established within the UK. Careful research is conducted into the historical background, health and temperament of any new breed before Kennel Club recognition is granted. The Kennel Club currently recognises 196 breeds. Upon recognition, breeds are placed on the Imported Breed Register until they are deemed eligible for transferral to the Breed Register".
A standard provides a guideline for breeders and judges. It is something of an ideal that dogs of each breed must strive to match. With some breeds, dogs are already being bred that match the ideal. Other breeds have a long way to go. There is a list of defects for each breed. These can be serious defects that disqualify the dog, in which case it will be excluded from breeding. Permitted defects are not serious, but do cost points in a show.

The breed standard for the Labrador Retriever

General Appearance

Strongly built, short-coupled, very active; broad in skull; broad and deep through chest and ribs; broad and strong over loins and hindquarters.

Characteristics

Good-tempered, very agile. Excellent nose, soft mouth; keen love of water. Adaptable, devoted companion.

Yellow

Temperament
Intelligent, keen and biddable, with a strong will to please. Kindly nature, with no trace of aggression or undue shyness.

Liver or chocolate

Head and Skull
Skull broad with defined stop; clean-cut without fleshy cheeks. Jaws of medium length, powerful not snipy. Nose wide, nostrils well developed.

Eyes
Medium size, expressing intelligence and good temper; brown or hazel.

Ears
Not large or heavy, hanging close to head and set rather far back.

Mouth
Jaws and teeth strong with a perfect, regular and complete scissor bite, i.e. upper teeth closely overlapping lower teeth and set square to the jaws.

Neck
Clean, strong, powerful, set into well placed shoulders.

Forequarters
Shoulders long and sloping. Forelegs well boned and straight from elbow to ground when viewed from either front or side.

Body
Chest of good width and depth, with well sprung barrel ribs. Level topline. Loins wide, short-coupled and strong.

Hindquarters
Well developed, not sloping to tail; well turned stifle. Hocks well let down, cowhocks highly undesirable.

Feet
Round, compact; well arched toes and well developed pads.

Tail
Distinctive feature, very thick towards base, gradually tapering towards tip, medium length, free from feathering, but clothed thickly all round with short, thick, dense coat, thus giving 'rounded' appearance described as 'Otter' tail. May be carried gaily but should not curl over back.

Gait/Movement
Free, covering adequate ground; straight and true in front and rear.

Coat
Distinctive feature, short dense without wave or feathering, giving fairly hard feel to the touch; weather-resistant undercoat.

Colour
Wholly black, yellow or liver/ chocolate. Yellows range from light cream to red fox. Small white spot on chest permissible.

Size
Ideal height at withers:
dogs: 56-57 cms (22-221/2 ins);
bitches: 55-56 cms (211/2-22 ins).

Faults
Any departure from the foregoing points should be considered a fault and the seriousness with which the fault should be regarded should be in exact proportion to its degree.

Note
Male animals should have two apparently normal testicles fully descended into the scrotum.

Breed standard by courtesy of the Kennel Club of Great Britain

Black

Buying a Labrador Retriever

Once you've made that properly considered decision to buy a dog, there are several options. Should it be a puppy, an adult dog, or even an older dog?

Should it be a bitch or dog, a pedigree dog or a cross? Of course, the question also comes up as to where to buy your dog - from a private person, a reliable breeder or an animal shelter? For you and the animal, it's vital to get these questions sorted out in advance. You want a dog that will fit your circumstances properly. With a puppy, you get a playful energetic housemate that will easily adapt to a new environment. If you want something quieter, an older dog is a good choice.

Pros and cons of the Labrador

A Labrador retriever is not only a hunting dog, but also makes a fine pet. Both characteristics form this breed and both need their own, correct approach.

A Labrador possesses the urge to retrieve from a very early age. You can do your dog no greater favour than to let it search for objects and bring them back to you. If you don't play on this characteristic, your dog will become bored, and mischief is usually the consequence. A Labrador only feels happy when together with people. Being left alone frequently will spoil its character. It is also a real 'working dog' with a strong *will to please*. It will regard following a training course as a splendid outing.

Because a (young) Labrador is definitely not a dog you buy and forget, keep the following in mind: Why have you chosen a hunting dog; why a Labrador and not another shorthaired breed? Are you willing to carry your puppy up and down the stairs for the first six months? If you're absolutely sure that you want a Labrador, then it will help you to know that the liver (or chocolate) coloured varieties is very scarce and that the waiting time for these dogs is longer than for the other colourings.

Male or female?

The decision whether to buy a male or female, a dog or bitch, is entirely a personal one. A male Labrador is somewhat bigger and stronger than the female. It also urinates more. Compared to the female he displays somewhat different character traits, he is more affectionate for instance. These differences are particularly pronounced during puberty, so a good upbringing is very important. Otherwise you may end up with a strong, self-willed Labrador that can't be restrained in the vicinity of a female on heat.

A male typically needs more leadership because he tends to be more dominant by nature. He will try to play boss over other dogs and, if he gets the chance, over people too. In the wild, the most dominant dog (or wolf) is always the leader of the pack. In many cases this is a male. A bitch is much more focussed on her master, she sees him as the pack leader. A puppy test is good for defining the kind of character a young dog will develop. During a test one usually sees that a dog is more dominant than a bitch. You can often quickly recognise the bossy, the adventurous and the cautious characters. So visit the litter a couple of times early on. Try to pick a puppy that suits your own personality. A dominant dog, for instance, needs a strong hand. It will often try to see how far it can go. You must regularly make it clear who's the boss, and that it must obey all the members of the family.

When bitches are sexually mature, they will go into season. On average, a bitch is in season twice a year for about two or three weeks. This is the fertile period when she can become pregnant. Particularly in the second half of her season, she will want to go looking for a dog to mate with. A male dog will show more masculine traits once he is sexually mature. He will make sure other dogs know what territory is his by urinating as often as possible in as many places as he can. He is also difficult to restrain if there's a bitch in season nearby. As far as normal care is concerned there is little difference between a dog and a bitch.

Puppy or adult?

After you've made the decision for a male or female, the next

question comes up. Should it be a puppy or an adult dog? Your household circumstances usually play a major role here.

Of course, it's great having a sweet little puppy in the house, but bringing up a young dog requires a lot of time. In the first year of its life it learns more than during the rest of its life. This is the period when the foundations are laid for elementary matters such as house-training, obedience and social behaviour. You must reckon with the fact that your puppy will keep you busy for a couple of hours a day, certainly in the first few months. You won't need so much time with a grown dog. It has already been brought up, but this doesn't mean it doesn't need correcting from time to time.

A puppy will no doubt leave a trail of destruction in its wake for the first few months. With a little bad luck, this will cost you a number of rolls of wallpaper, some good shoes and a few socks. In the worst case you'll be left with some chewed furniture. Some puppies even manage to tear curtains from their rails. With good upbringing this 'vandalism' will quickly disappear, but you won't have to worry about this if you get an older dog.

The greatest advantage of a puppy, of course, is that you can bring it up your own way. And the upbringing a dog gets (or doesn't get) is a major influence on its whole character. Finally, financial aspects may play a role in your choice. A puppy is generally (much) more expensive than an adult dog, not only in purchase price but also in 'maintenance'. A puppy needs to go to the vet's more often for the necessary vaccinations and check-ups.

Overall, bringing up a puppy involves a good deal of energy, time and money, but you have its upbringing in your own hands. An adult dog costs less money and time, but its character is already formed. You should also try to find out about the background of an adult dog. Its previous owner may have formed its character in somewhat less positive ways.

Two dogs?

Having two or more dogs in the house is not just nice for us, but also for the animals themselves. Dogs get a lot of pleasure from company of their own kind. After all, they are pack animals.

If you're sure that you want two young dogs, it's best not to buy them at the same time. Bringing a dog up and establishing the bond between dog and master takes time, and you need to give a lot of attention to your dog in this phase. Having two puppies in the house means you have to divide your attention between them too much. Apart from that, there's a danger that they will focus on one another rather than on their master. Buy the second pup when the first is (almost) an adult.

Two adult dogs can normally be brought into the house together quite easily as long as they know each other. If this is not the case, then you need to give them the opportunity to get to know each other. This is best achieved by letting the dogs get to know each other on neutral ground. This way you will avoid that one of the dogs will try to defend its territory. On neutral territory, an acquaintance's garden where neither dog has been before, for example, both dogs are basically equal. Once they got to know each other, you can take them home where they can sort out the hierarchy amongst themselves.

Do not be tempted to intervene in 'squabbles'. This is a human urge, but for the dog higher up in the hierarchy it is as if its position is being undone. This will cause it to display even more dominant behaviour with all the nasty consequences. Once the hierarchy has been established, most dogs will usually get along very well.

Getting a puppy when the first dog is somewhat older often has a positive effect on the older dog. The influence of the puppy almost seems to give it a second childhood. The older dog, if it's been well brought up, can help with the upbringing of the puppy, as young dogs like to imitate the behaviour of their elders. Don't

forget to give both dogs the same amount of attention. Take them both for separate walks at least once per day during the first eighteen months. Make sure the older dog has enough opportunities to get some peace and quiet. It won't always be able to keep up with the speed of such an enthusiastic youngster. A puppy also needs to sleep a lot and thus might need to have the brakes put on once in a while.

The combination of dog and bitch needs special attention. It is advisable to get two dogs of the same sex, as this will prevent a lot of problems. Sterilisation or castration is, of course, a solution to prevent unwanted offspring, but it is a final one. A castrated or sterilised animal will never be able to reproduce again.

A dog and children

Dogs and children are a great combination. They can play together and get great pleasure out of each other's company. Moreover, children need to learn how to handle living beings; they develop respect and a sense of responsibility by caring for a dog (or other pets). However sweet a dog is, children must understand that it is an animal and not a toy. A dog isn't comfortable when it's being messed around with. It can become frightened, timid and even aggressive. So make it clear what a dog likes and what it doesn't. Look for ways the child can play with the dog, perhaps a game of hide and seek where the child hides and the dog has to find it. Even a simple tennis ball can give enormous pleasure. Children must learn to leave a dog in peace when it doesn't want to play any more. The dog must also have its own place where it's not disturbed. Have children help with your dog's care as much as possible. A strong bond will be the result.

The arrival of a baby also means changes in the life of a dog. Before the birth you can help get the dog acquainted with the new situation. Let it sniff at the new things in the house and it will quickly accept them. When the baby has arrived involve the dog as much as possible in day-by-day events, but make sure it gets plenty of attention too. **Never** leave a dog alone with young children. Crawling infants sometimes make unexpected movements, which can easily frighten a dog. And infants are hugely curious, and may try to find out whether the tail is really fastened to the dog, or whether its eyes come out, just like they do with their cuddly toys. But a dog is a dog and it will defend itself when it feels threatened.

Where to buy

There are various ways of acquiring a dog. The decision for a puppy or an adult dog will also define for the most part where to buy your dog.

If it's to be a puppy, then you need to find a breeder with a litter. If you chose a popular breed like the Labrador Retriever, there is choice enough. But you may also face the problem that there are so many puppies on sale that have only been bred for profit's sake. You can see how many puppies are for sale by looking in the regional newspaper every Saturday. Some of these dogs have a pedigree, but many don't. These breeders often don't watch out for breed-specific illnesses and any hereditary breeding faults and defects; puppies are separated from their mother as fast as possible and are thus insufficiently socialised. Never buy a puppy that is too young, or whose mother you weren't able to see.

Fortunately there are also enough bona-fide breeders of Labrador Retrievers. Try to visit a number of breeders before you actually buy your puppy. Ask if the breeder is prepared to help you after you've bought your puppy, and to help you find solutions for any problems that may come up.

A breeder that feels responsible for his breed will never mate parent dogs suffering from a congenital condition. Breeders that are members of the breed association are expelled if they do use such animals. But there are plenty of breeders that are not association members. They don't have to stick to the breeding regulations and, in principle, can also breed with unhealthy animals. A reliable breeder can also face problems with congenital conditions within his population, of course, but if he works according to the breed association guidelines, this is a guarantee for a minimal risk. Especially when buying such a popular dog as the Labrador Retriever, it can not be overstated how extremely

important it is to contact (via a breeders club) a good, reliable breeder!

If you're looking for an adult dog, it's best to contact the breed association, who often help place adult dogs that can no longer be kept by their owners because of personal circumstances (impulse buying, moving home, divorce etc.). You can also try an animal shelter, but the chances are you'll have to search for some time, because animal shelters don't keep 'stocks' of certain breeds.

Finally, you must realise that a pedigree is nothing more or less than a proof of descent. Most kennel clubs also issue pedigrees to the offspring of parents that suffer from a congenital condition, or that have never been checked for them. A pedigree says nothing about the health of the parent dogs or of your puppy.

Things to watch out for

Buying a puppy is no simple matter. You must pay attention to the following:

1. Never buy a puppy on impulse, even if it is love at first sight. A dog is a living being that will need care and attention over a long period. It is not a toy that you can put away when you're done with it.
2. Take a good look at the mother. Is she calm, nervous, aggressive, well cared for or neglected? The behaviour and condition of the mother is not only a sign of the quality of the breeder, but also of the puppy you're about to buy.
3. Avoid buying a puppy whose mother has been kept only in a kennel. A young dog needs as many different impressions as possible in its first few months, including living in a family group. It gets used to people and possibly other pets. Kennel dogs miss these experiences and are inadequately socialised.
4. Always ask to see the parents' papers (vaccination certificates, pedigrees).
5. Both parents should have been x-rayed for potential hip or elbow dysplasia, and they should have an official certificate to prove it.
6. The eyes of both parents should have been checked for any congenital eye disorders, and have an examination certificate, which should not

be older than one year.
7. The mother should not have had more than five litters. Check this with the breeder or the breed association (you can find the address at the back of this book).
8. Never buy a puppy younger than eight weeks.
9. Put all agreements with the breeder in writing. A model agreement is available from the Kennel Club.

Ten golden puppy rules

1. Walk your puppy in doses followed by one hour play, a feed and then three hours sleep.
2. Don't let your puppy run endlessly after a ball or stick.
3. Don't let your puppy romp wildly with large, heavy dogs.
4. Never let your puppy play on a full tummy.
5. Don't give your puppy anything to drink straight after a meal.
6. Don't let your puppy walk up and down steps for the first year. Be careful with shiny floors.
7. Don't add supplements to ready-made food.
8. Watch out for your puppy's weight. Being overweight can lead to bone abnormalities.
9. Give your puppy a quiet place to sleep.
10. Pick your puppy up carefully, one hand under its chest, the other under its hindquarters.

Travelling with your Labrador

There are a few things to think about before travelling with your dog.

While one dog may enjoy travelling, another may hate it. You may like holidays in far-away places, but it's questionable whether your dog will enjoy them as much.

That very first trip

The first trip of a puppy's life is also the most nerve-wrecking. This is the trip from the breeder's to its new home. If possible, pick up your puppy in the morning. It then has the whole day to get used to the new situation. Ask the breeder not to feed it that day. The young animal will be overwhelmed by all kinds of new experiences. Firstly, it's away from its mother; it's in a small room (the car) with all its different smells, noises and strange people. So there's a big chance that the puppy will be car-sick this first time, with the annoying consequence that it will remember travelling in the car as an unpleasant experience.

So it's important to make this first trip as pleasant as possible. When picking up a puppy, always take someone with you who can sit in the back seat with the puppy on his or her lap and talk to it calmly. If it's too warm for the puppy, a place on the floor at the feet of your companion is ideal. The pup will lie there relatively quietly and may even take a nap. Ask the breeder for a cloth or something else from the puppies' basket or bed that carries a familiar scent. The puppy can lie on this in the car, and it will also help if it feels lonely during the first nights at home.

If the trip home is a long one, then stop for a break (once in a while). Let your puppy roam and sniff around (on the lead!), have a little drink and, if necessary, do its business. Do take care to lay an old towel in the car. It can happen that the puppy, in its nervousness, may urinate or be sick. It's also good advice to give a puppy positive experiences with car journeys. Make short trips to nice places where you can walk and play with it. It can be a real nuisance if your dog doesn't like travelling in a car. After all, once in a while you will have to take it to certain places, such as the vet's or to visit friends and acquaintances.

Taking your Labrador Retriever on holiday

When making holiday plans, you also need to think about what you're going to do with your dog during that time. Are you taking it with you, putting it into kennels or leaving it with friends? In any event there are a number of things you need to do in good time. If you want to take your dog with you, you need to be sure in

advance that it will be welcome at your holiday home, and what rules there are. If you're going abroad it will need certain vaccinations and a health certificate, which normally need to be done four weeks before departure. You must also be sure that you've made all the arrangements necessary to bring your dog back home to the UK, without it needing to go into quarantine under the rabies regulations. Your vet can give you the most recent information.

If your trip is to southern Europe, ask for a treatment against ticks (you can read more about this in the chapter on parasites).

Although dog-owners usually enjoy taking their dog on holiday, you must seriously ask yourself whether the dog feels that way too. Labradors certainly don't always feel comfortable in a hot country. Days spent travelling in a car are also often not their preference, and some dogs suffer badly from car-sickness. There are good medicines for this, but it's questionable whether you're doing your dog a favour with them. If you do decide to take it with you, make regular stops at safe places during your journey, so that your dog can have a good run. Take plenty of fresh drinking water with you, as well as the food your dog is used to. Don't leave your dog in a car that is standing in the sun. It can quickly be overcome by the heat, with even fatal consequences. If you can't avoid it, park the car in the shade if at all possible, and leave a window open for a little fresh air. Even if you've taken these precautions, never stay away long!

If you're travelling by plane or ship, make sure in good time that your dog can travel with you and what rules you need to observe. You will need some time to make all the arrangements. Maybe you decide not to take your dog with you, and you then need to find somewhere for it to stay. Arrangements for a place in kennels need to be made well in advance, and there may be certain vaccinations required, which need to be given a minimum of one month before the stay.

If your dog can't be accommodated in the homes of relatives or friends, it might be possible to have an acquaintance stay in your house. This also needs to be arranged well in advance, as it may be difficult to find someone who can do this.

Always ensure that your dog can be traced should it run away or get lost while on holiday. A little tube with your address or a tag with home and holiday address can avoid a lot of problems.

Moving home

Dogs generally become more attached to humans than to the house they live in. Moving home is usually not a problem for them. But it can be useful before moving to let the dog get to know its new home and the area around it.

If you can, leave your dog with relatives or friends (or in kennels) on the day of the move. The chance of it running away or getting lost is then practically non-existent. When your move is complete, you can pick up your dog and let it quietly get familiar with its new home and environment. Give it its own place in the house at once and it will quickly adapt. During the first week or so, always walk your dog on a lead because an animal can also get lost in new surroundings. Always take a different route so it quickly gets to know the neighbourhood.

Don't forget to get your new address and phone number engraved on the dog's tag. Send a change of address notice to the chip or tattoo registration office. Dogs must sometimes be registered in a new community.

Feeding your Labrador

A dog will actually eat a lot more than just meat. In the wild it would eat its prey complete with skin and fur, including the bones, stomach and the innards with their semi-digested vegetable material.

In this way the dog supplements its meat menu with the vitamins and minerals it needs. This is also the basis for feeding a domestic dog.

Ready-made foods

It's not easy for a layman to put together a complete menu for a dog, which includes all the necessary proteins, fats, vitamins and minerals in just the right proportions and quantities. Meat alone is certainly not a complete meal for a dog. It contains too little calcium. A calcium deficiency over time can lead to bone defects, and for a fast-growing puppy this can lead to serious skeletal deformities.

If you mix its food yourself, you can easily give your dog too much in terms of vitamins and minerals, which can also be bad for your dog's health. You can avoid these problems by giving it ready-made food of a good brand. These products are well-balanced and contain everything your dog needs, so supplements are superfluous. The amount of food your dog needs depends on its weight and activity level. You can find guidelines on the packaging. Split the food into two meals per day if possible, and always ensure there's a dish of fresh drinking water next to its food.

Give your dog the time to digest its food, don't let it outside straight after a meal.

Because the nutritional needs of a dog vary depending on its age and way of life, there is now a whole range of dog food available. There are "light" foods for less active dogs, "energy" foods for working or hunting dogs and "senior" foods for the older dog.

Canned foods, mixer and dry foods

Ready-made foods available at pet shops or in the supermarket can roughly be split into canned food, mixer and dry food. Whichever form you choose, ensure that it's a complete food with all the necessary ingredients. You can see this on the packaging.

Most dogs love canned food. Although the better brands are composed well, they do have one disadvantage: they are soft. A dog fed only on canned food will sooner or later have problems with its teeth (plaque, paradontosis). Besides canned food, give your dog hard foods at certain times or a dog chew, such as Nylabone Healthy Edibles.

Mixer is a food consisting of chunks, dried vegetables and grains. Almost all moisture has been extracted. The advantages of mixer are that it is light and keeps well. You add a certain amount of water and the meal is ready. A disadvantage is that it must definitely not be fed without water. Without the extra fluid, mixer will absorb the fluids present in the stomach, with serious results. Should your dog manage to get at the bag and enjoy its contents, you must immediately give it plenty to drink.

Dry chunks have also had the moisture extracted but not as much as mixer. The advantage of dry foods is that they are hard, forcing the dog to use its jaws, removing plaque and massaging the gums.

Dog chew products

Of course, once in a while you want to spoil your dog with something extra. Don't give it pieces of cheese or sausage as these contain too much salt and fat. There are various products available that a dog will find delicious and which are also healthy, especially for its teeth. You'll find a large range of varying quality in the pet shop.

The butcher's left-overs

The bones of slaughtered animals have traditionally been given to the dog, and dogs are crazy about them, but they are not without risks. Pork and poultry bones are too weak. They can splinter and cause serious injury to the intestines. Beef bones are more

suitable, but they must first be cooked to kill off dangerous bacteria. Pet shops carry a range of smoked, cooked and dried abattoir residue, such as pigs' ears, bull penis, tripe sticks, oxtails, gullet, dried muscle meat, and hoof chews.

Fresh meat

If you do want to give your dog fresh meat occasionally, never give it raw, but always boiled or roasted. Raw (or not fully cooked) pork or chicken can contain life-threatening bacteria. Chicken can be contaminated by the notorious salmonella bacteria, while pork can carry the Aujeszky virus. This disease is incurable and will quickly lead to the death of your pet.

Buffalo hide or cowhide chews

Dog chews are mostly made of beef or buffalo hide. Chews are usually knotted or pressed hide and can come in the form of little shoes, twisted sticks, lollies, balls and various other shapes; nice to look at and a nice change.

Munchie sticks

Munchie sticks are green, yellow, red or brown coloured sticks of various thickness. They consist of ground buffalo hide with a number of often undefined additives. The composition and quality of these between-meal treats is not always clear. Some are fine, but there have also been sticks found to contain high levels of cardboard and even paint residues. Choose a product whose ingredients are clearly described.

Overweight?

Recent investigations have shown that many dogs are overweight. A dog usually gets too fat because of over-feeding and lack of exercise.

Use of medicines or a disease is rarely the cause. Dogs that get too fat are often given too much food or too many treats between meals. Gluttony or boredom can also be a cause, and a dog often puts on weight following castration or sterilisation. Due to changes in hormone levels it becomes less active and consumes less energy. Finally, simply too little exercise alone can lead to a dog becoming overweight.

You can use the following rule of thumb to check whether your dog is overweight: you should be able to feel its ribs, but not see them. If you can't feel its ribs then your dog is much too fat. Overweight dogs live a passive life, they play too little and tire quickly. They also suffer from all kinds of medical problems (problems in joints and heart conditions). They usually die younger too.

So it's important to make sure your dog doesn't get too fat. Always follow the guidelines on food packaging. Adapt them if your dog is less active or gets lots of snacks. Try to make sure your dog gets plenty of exercise by playing and running with it as much as you can. If your dog starts to show signs of putting on weight you can switch to a low-calorie food. If it's really too fat and reducing its food quantity doesn't help, then a special diet is the only solution.

Caring for your Labrador

Good (daily) care is extremely important for your dog. A well cared for dog is less likely to become ill.

Caring for your dog is not only necessary but also a pleasure. Master and dog are giving each other some attention, and it's an excellent opportunity for a game and a cuddle.

The coat

Caring for your dog's coat involves regular brushing and combing, together with checking for parasites such as fleas. How often a dog needs to be brushed and combed depends on the length of its coat. For a shorthaired breed like the Labrador, once or twice a week is sufficient. Use the right equipment for taking care of the coat. Combs should not be too sharp and you should use a rubber or natural hairbrush. Always comb from the head back towards the tail, following the direction of the hair.
If you get a puppy used to being brushed from an early age, it will enjoy having its coat cared for. Only bathe a dog when it's really necessary. Always use a special dog shampoo and make sure it doesn't get into the dog's eyes or ears. Rinse the suds out thoroughly. Only let your dog outside again when it's totally dry; dogs can catch a cold too!

A vet can prescribe special medicinal shampoos for some skin conditions. Always follow the instructions to the letter.

Good flea prevention is highly important to avoid skin and coat problems. Fleas must be treated not only on the dog itself but also in its surroundings (see the chapter on parasites). Coat problems can also occur due to an allergy to certain food substances. In such cases, a vet can prescribe a hypo-allergenic diet.

Teeth

A dog must be able to eat properly to stay in good condition, so it needs healthy teeth. Check its teeth regularly. Get in touch with your vet if you suspect that all is not well. Regular feeds of hard dry food can help keep your dog's teeth clean and healthy. There are special dog chews, such as Nylabone, on the market that help prevent plaque and help keep the animal's breath fresh.

What really helps is to regularly brush your dog's teeth. You can use special toothbrushes for dogs, but a finger wrapped in a small piece of gauze will also do the job. Get your dog used to having its teeth cleaned at an early age and you won't have problems.

You can even teach an older dog to have its teeth cleaned. With a dog chew as a reward it will certainly be happy.

Nails

On a dog that regularly walks on hard surfaces, its nails usually grind themselves down. In this case there's no need to clip their nails. But it wouldn't do any harm to check their length now and again, especially on dogs that don't get out on the streets often. Using a piece of paper, you can easily see whether its nails are too long. If you can push the paper between the nail and the ground when the dog is standing, then the nail is the right length.

Nails that are too long can bother a dog. It can injure itself when scratching, so they must be kept trimmed. You can buy special nail clippers in pet shops. Be careful not to clip back too far as you could damage the skin around the nail, which can bleed profusely. If you feel unsure, have this necessary task done by a vet or a professional groomer.

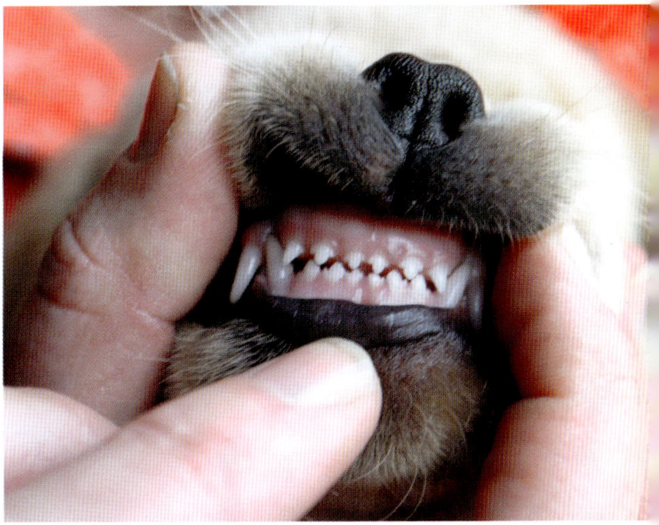

Special attention is needed for the nail on the side of the rear paws, also called the dew claw. This nail never touches the ground, and never grinds down. Clip this nail back regularly, otherwise your dog can get caught on it.

Eyes

A dog's eyes should be cleaned regularly. Discharge gets into the corners of the eye. You can easily remove it by wiping it downward with your thumb. If you don't like doing that, use a piece of tissue or toilet paper.

Keeping your dog's eyes clean will take only a few seconds a day, so do it every day. If the discharge becomes yellow this could point to an irritation or infection. Eye drops (from your vet) will quickly solve this problem.

Ears

The ears are often forgotten when caring for dogs, but they must be checked at least once a week. If its ears are very dirty or have too much wax, you must clean them. This should preferably be done with a clean cotton cloth, moistened with lukewarm water or baby oil. Cotton wool is not suitable due to the fluff it can leave behind. **Never** enter the ear canal with an object.

If hairs in the ear do cause problems, then it's better to remove them. Carefully pull them out using your thumb and index finger.

If you do neglect cleaning your dog's ears there's a substantial risk of infection. A dog that is constantly scratching at its ears might be suffering from dirty ears, an ear infection or ear mites, making a visit to the vet essential.

Bringing up your Labrador

It is very important that your dog is properly brought up and is obedient. Not only will this bring you more pleasure, but it's also nicer for your environment.

A puppy can learn what it may and may not do by playing. Rewards and consistency are important tools in bringing up a dog. Reward it with your voice, a stroke or something tasty and it will quickly learn to obey. A puppy training course can also help you along the way.

(Dis)obedience

A dog that won't obey you is not just a problem for you, but also for your surroundings. Even though a Labrador is known for its friendly character and its strong will to please, it remains a hunting dog (with all the associated instincts). You must teach it some basic rules. The Labrador is a dog that loves to learn, so this shouldn't present too many problems.
It's important to avoid unwanted behaviour. In fact, this is what training your dog is all about, so get started early. 'Start 'em young!' applies to dogs too. An untrained dog is not just a nuisance, but can also cause dangerous situations by running into the road, chasing joggers or jumping at people. A dog must be trained out of this undesirable behaviour as quickly as possible. The longer you let it go on, the more difficult it will become to correct. The best thing to do is to attend a special obedience course. This won't only help to

correct the dog's behaviour, but its owner also learns how to handle undesirable behaviour at home. A dog must not only obey its master during training, but at home too.

Always be consistent when training good behaviour and correcting annoying behaviour. This means a dog may always behave in a certain way, or must never behave that way. Reward it for good behaviour and never punish it after the fact for any wrongdoing. If your dog finally comes after you've been calling it a long time, then reward it. If you're angry because you had to wait so long, it may feel it's actually being punished for coming. It will probably not obey at all the next time for fear of punishment.

Try to take no notice of undesirable behaviour. Your dog will perceive your reaction (even a negative one) as a reward for this behaviour. If you need to correct the dog, then do this immediately. Use your voice or grip it by the scruff of its neck and push it to the ground. This is the way a mother dog calls her pups to order. Rewards for good behaviour are, by far, preferable to punishment; they always get a better result.

House-training

The very first training (and one of the most important) that a dog needs is house-training. The basis for good house-training is keeping a good eye on your puppy. If you pay attention, you will notice that it will sniff a long time and do turns around a certain spot before doing its business there. Pick it up gently and place it outside, always at the same place. Reward it abundantly if it does its business there.

Another good moment for house-training is after eating or sleeping. A puppy often needs to do its business at these times. Let it relieve itself before playing with it, otherwise it will forget to do so and you'll not reach your goal. For the first few days, take your puppy out for a walk just after it's eaten or woken up. It will quickly learn the meaning, especially if it's rewarded with a dog biscuit for a successful attempt. Of course, it's not always possible to go out after every snack or snooze. Lay newspapers at different spots in the house. Whenever the pup needs to do its business, place it on a newspaper. After some time it will start to look for a place itself. Then start to reduce the number of newspapers until there is just one left, at the front or back door. The puppy will learn to go to the door if it needs to relieve itself. Then you put it on the lead and go out with it. Finally you can remove the last newspaper. Your puppy is now house-trained.

One thing that certainly won't work is punishing an accident

after the fact. A dog whose nose is rubbed in its urine or its droppings won't understand that at all. It will only get frightened of you. Rewarding works much better than punishment. An indoor kennel or cage can be a good tool to help in house-training. A puppy won't foul its own nest, so a kennel can be a good solution for the night, or during periods in the day when you can't watch it. But a kennel must not become a prison where your dog is locked up day and night.

First exercises

The basic commands for an obedient dog are those for sit, lie down, come and stay. But a puppy should first learn its name. Use it as much as possible from the first day on followed by a friendly 'Come!'. Reward it with your voice and a stroke when it comes to you. Your puppy will quickly recognise the intention and has now learned its first command in a playful manner. Don't appear too strict towards a young puppy, and don't always punish it immediately if it doesn't always react in the right way. When you call your puppy to you in this way have it come right to you. You can teach a pup to sit by holding a piece of dog biscuit above its nose and then slowly moving it backwards. The puppy's head will also move backwards until its hind legs slowly go down. At that moment you call 'Sit!'. After a few attempts, it will quickly know this nice game. Use the 'Sit!' command before you give your dog its food, put it on the lead, or before it's allowed to cross the street.

Teaching the command to lie down is similar. Instead of moving the piece of dog biscuit backwards, move it down vertically until your hand reaches the ground and then forwards. The dog will also move its forepaws forwards and lie down on its own. At that moment call 'Lie down!' or 'Lay!'. This command is useful when you want a dog to be quiet.

Two people are needed for the 'Come!' command. One holds the dog back while the other runs away. After about fifteen metres, he stops and enthusiastically calls 'Come!'. The other person now lets the dog go, and it should obey the command at once. Again you reward it abundantly. The 'Come!' command is useful in many situations and good for safety too.

A dog learns to stay from the sitting or lying position. While it's sitting or lying down, you give the command 'Stay!' and then step back one step. If the dog moves with you, quietly put it back in position, without displaying anger. If you do react angrily, you're actually punishing it for coming to you, and you'll only confuse your dog. It can't understand that coming is

rewarded one time, and punished another. Once the dog stays nicely, reward it abundantly. Practise this exercise with increasing distances (at first no more than one metre). The 'Stay!' command is useful when getting out of the car.

Courses

Obedience courses to help you bring up your dog are available across the country. These courses are not just informative, but also fun for dog and master.

With a puppy, you can begin with a puppy course. This is designed to provide the basic training. A puppy that has attended such a course has learned about all kinds of things that will confront it in later life: other dogs, humans, traffic and what these mean. The puppy will also learn obedience and to follow a number of basic commands. Apart from all that, attention will be given to important subjects such as brushing, being alone, travelling in a car, and doing its business in the right places.

The next step after a puppy course is a course for young dogs. This course repeats the basic exercises and ensures that the growing dog doesn't get into bad habits. After this, the dog can move on to an obedience course for full-grown dogs. For more information on where to find

courses in your area, contact your local kennel club. You can get its address from the Kennel Club of Great Britain in London. In some areas, the RSPCA organises obedience classes and your local branch may be able to give you information.

Play and toys

There are various ways to play with your dog. You can romp and run with it, but also play a number of games, such as retrieving, tug-of-war, hide-and-seek and catch. A tennis ball is ideal for retrieving, you can play tug-of-war with an old sock or a special tugging rope. Start with tug-of-war only when your dog is a year old. A puppy must first get its second teeth and then they need several months to strengthen. There's a real chance of your dog's teeth becoming deformed if you start too young. You can use almost anything for a game of hide-and-seek. A frisbee is ideal for catching games. Never use too small a ball for games. It can easily get lodged into the dog's throat.

Play is extremely important. Not only does it strengthen the bond between dog and master, but it's also healthy for both. Make sure that you're the one that ends the game. Only stop when the dog has brought back the ball or frisbee, and make sure you always win the tug-of-war. This confirms your dominant position in the hierarchy. Use these toys only during play so that the dog doesn't forget their significance. When choosing a special dog toy, remember that dogs are hardly careful with them. So always buy toys of good quality that a dog can't easily destroy.
Be very careful with sticks and twigs. The latter, particularly, can easily splinter. A splinter of wood in your dog's throat or intestines can cause awful problems. Throwing sticks or twigs can also be dangerous. If they stick into the ground a dog can easily run into them with an open mouth.

If you would like to do more than just play games, you can now also play sports with your dog. For people who want to do more, there are various other sporting alternatives such as Flyball, Agility and Obedience.

Aggressiveness

Labradors are practically never aggressive or unusually timid. But in exceptional cases, even they can sometimes be difficult with other animals or people, so it's good to understand more about the background of aggression in dogs.

There are two different types of aggressive behaviour: The anxious-aggressive dog and the dominant-aggressive dog. An anxious-aggressive dog can be recognised by its pulled back ears and its low position. It will have pulled in its lips, baring its teeth. This dog is aggressive because it's very frightened and feels cornered. It would prefer to run away, but if it can't then it will bite to defend itself. It will grab its victim anywhere it can. The attack is usually brief and, as soon as the dog can see a way to escape, it's gone. In a confrontation with other dogs, it will normally turn out as the loser. It can become even more aggressive once it's realised that people or other dogs are afraid of it. This behaviour cannot be corrected just like that. First you have to try and understand what the dog is afraid of. Professional advice is a good idea here because the wrong approach can easily make the problem worse.

The dominant-aggressive dog's body language is different. Its ears stand up and its tail is raised and stiff. This dog will always go for its victim's arms, legs or throat. It is extremely self-assured and highly placed in the dog hierarchy. Its attack is a display of power rather than a consequence of fear. This dog needs to know who's boss. You must bring it up rigorously and with a strong hand. An obedience course can help.

A dog may also bite because it's in pain. This is a natural defensive reaction. In this case try to resolve

the dog's fear as far as possible. Reward it for letting you get to the painful spot. Be careful, because a dog in pain may also bite its master! Muzzling it can help prevent problems if you have to do something that may be painful. Never punish a dog for this type of aggression!

Fear

The source of anxious behaviour can often be traced to the first weeks of a dog's life. A shortage of new experiences during this important phase (also called the 'socialisation phase') has great influence on its later behaviour.
A dog that never encountered humans, other dogs or animals during the socialisation phase will be afraid of them later. This fear is common in dogs brought up in a barn or kennel, with almost no contact with humans. As we saw, fear can lead to aggressive behaviour, so it's important that a puppy gets as many new impressions as possible in the first weeks of its life. Take it with you into town in the car or on the bus, walk it down busy streets and allow it to have plenty of contact with people, other dogs and other animals.
It's a huge task to turn an anxious, poorly socialised dog into a real pet. It will probably take an enormous amount of attention, love, patience and energy to get such an animal used to everything around it. Reward it often and give it plenty of time to adapt and, over time, it will learn to trust you and become less anxious. Try not to force anything, because that will always have the reverse effect. Here too, an obedience course can help a lot. A dog can be especially afraid of strangers. Have visitors give it something tasty as a treat. Put a can of dog biscuits by the door so that your visitors can spoil your dog when they arrive. Here again, don't try to force anything. If the dog is still frightened, leave it in peace.

Dogs are often frightened in certain situations; well-known examples are thunderstorms and fireworks. In these cases try to ignore their anxious behaviour. If you react to their whimpering and whining, it's the same as rewarding it. If you ignore its fear completely, the dog will quickly learn that nothing is wrong. You can speed up this 'learning process' by rewarding its positive behaviour.

Rewarding

Rewarding forms the basis for bringing up a dog. Rewarding good behaviour works far better than punishing bad behaviour and rewarding is also much more fun.

The opinions on how to bring up dogs have gradually changed. In the past the proper way to correct bad behaviour was a sharp pull on the lead. Today, experts view

rewards as a positive incentive to get dogs to do what we expect of them.

There are many ways to reward a dog. The usual ways are a stroke or a friendly word, even without a tasty treat to go with it. Of course, a piece of dog biscuit does wonders when you're training a puppy. Be sure you always have something delicious in your pocket to reward good behaviour.

Another form of reward is play. Any dog, but especially a Labrador, loves a game. Whenever a dog notices that you have a ball in your pocket, it won't go far from your side. As soon as you've finished playing, put the ball away. This way your dog will always do its best in exchange for a game. Despite the emphasis you put on rewarding good behaviour, a dog can sometimes be a nuisance or disobedient. You must correct such behaviour immediately. Always be consistent: once 'no' must always be 'no'.

Barking

Dogs which bark too much and too often are a nuisance for their surroundings. A dog-owner may tolerate barking up to a point, but neighbours are often annoyed by the unnecessary noise. Don't encourage your puppy to bark and yelp. Of course, it should be able to announce its presence, but if it goes on barking it must be called to order with a strict 'Quiet!'. If a puppy fails to obey, just hold its muzzle closed with your hand.

A dog will sometimes bark for long periods when left alone. It feels threatened and tries to get someone's attention by barking.

There are special training programmes for this problem, where dogs learn that being alone is nothing to be afraid of, and that their master will always return.

You can practise this with your dog at home. Leave the room and come back in at once. Reward your dog if it stays quiet. Gradually increase the length of your absences and keep rewarding it

as long as it remains quiet. Never punish the dog if it does bark or yelp. It will never understand punishment afterwards, and this will only make the problem worse. Never go back into the room as long as your dog is barking, as it will view this as a reward. You might want to make the dog feel more comfortable by switching the radio on for company during your absence. It will eventually learn that you always come back and the barking will reduce. If you don't get the required result, attend an obedience course.

Undesirable behaviour

Labrador retrievers are immensely friendly, enthusiastic dogs with a healthy appetite, but these positive traits can easily turn into negative ones.

Among Labradors, there are still some 'brutes' that can hardly be handled in their enthusiasm. Particularly a (heavily built) male can sometimes be problematic, and it's thus extremely important to bring up an overactive dog with a firm hand.

A Labrador is fixated on food, it sometimes seems as if they wolf the contents of their food bowl down without even looking what was in it. This healthy appetite can quickly turn into gluttony and begging. With its touching eyes, it can scrounge like no other dog, so you need to decide from the very first moment whether your dog may beg or not. Certainly, 'human' food is not good for dogs, but given in moderation and carefully it's no major problem. But, if you do, you're going to have a whimpering dog at the table whenever you sit down to eat.

If you decide you don't want your dog to beg, then be rigorous. Never give it anything at the table or from the sofa. Only put its food in its bowl and only feed it snacks at a certain fixed place, and never when it asks for one! Teach your dog to go to its basket whenever you're eating. Give it a dog biscuit as a reward. After a while it will automatically go to its basket as soon as you start laying the table or call 'dinner's ready!'. Of course it may only come out of its basket when everybody has got up from the table.

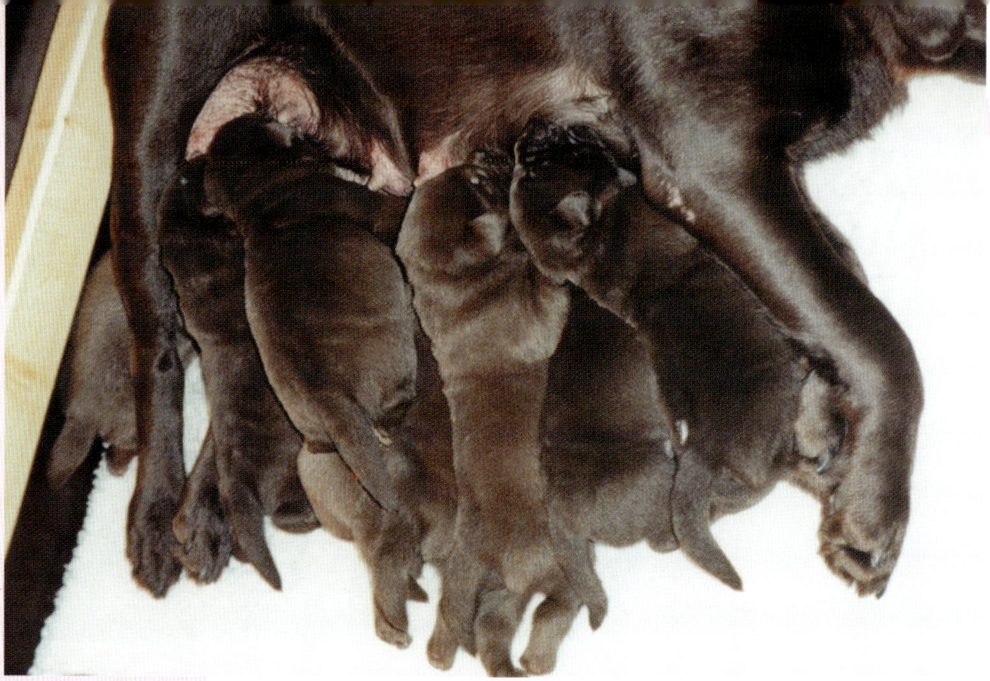

Breeding

Dogs, and thus Labrador Retrievers, follow their instincts, and one of nature's important processes is reproduction. For people who enjoy breeding dogs this is a positive circumstance.

Those who simply want a 'cosy companion' however, do not need the regular adventures with females on heat and unrestrainable males. Knowing a little about breeding dogs will help you to understand why they behave the way they do, and the measures you need to take when this happens.

Liability

Breeding dogs is much more than simply 1+1= many. If you're planning to breed with your Labrador, be on your guard, otherwise the whole affair can turn into a financial drama because, under the law, a breeder is liable for the 'quality' of his or her puppies.

The kennel clubs place strict conditions on animals used for breeding. They must be examined for possible congenital defects (see the chapter "Your Labrador Retriever's health"). This is the breeder's first obligation, and if you breed a litter and sell the puppies without these checks having been made, you can be held liable by the new owners for any costs arising from any inherited defects. These (veterinary) costs can be enormous! So contact the breed association if you plan to breed a litter of Labradors.

The female in season

Bitches become sexually mature at about eight to twelve months. Then they go into season for the first time. They are 'on heat' for two to three weeks. During this period they discharge little drops of blood and they are very attractive to males. The bitch is fertile during the second half of her season, and will accept a male to mate. The best time for mating is then between the ninth and thirteenth day of her season. A female's first season is often shorter and less severe than those that follow. If you do want to breed with your female you must allow this first (and sometimes the second) season to pass.

Most bitches go into season twice per year. If you do plan to breed with your Labrador in the future, then sterilisation is not an option to prevent unwanted offspring. A temporary solution is a contraceptive injection, although this is controversial because of side effects such as womb infections.

Phantom pregnancy

A phantom pregnancy is a not uncommon occurrence. The female behaves as if she has a litter. She takes all kinds of things to her basket and treats them like puppies. Her milk teats swell and sometimes milk is actually produced. The female will sometimes behave aggressively towards people or other animals, as if she is defending her young.

Phantom pregnancies usually begin two months after a season and can last a number of weeks. If it happens to a bitch once, it will often then occur after every season. If she suffers under it, sterilisation is the best solution, because continual phantom pregnancies increase the risk of womb or teat conditions. In the short term a hormone treatment is worth trying, perhaps also homeopathic medicines. Camphor spirit can give relief when teats are heavily swollen, but rubbing the teats with ice or a cold cloth (moisten and freeze) can also help relieve the pain. Feed the female less than usual, and make sure she gets enough attention and extra exercise.

Preparing to breed

If you do plan to breed a litter of puppies, you must first wait for your female to be physically and mentally full-grown. In any event you must let her first season pass. To mate a bitch, you need a male. You could simply let her out on the street and she will quickly return home pregnant. But if you have a pure-bred Labrador, then it certainly makes sense to mate her with the best possible candidate, even if she has no pedigree. Proceed with caution and think especially about the following: Accompanying a bitch through pregnancy, birth and the first eight to twelve weeks afterwards is a time-consuming affair. Never breed Labradors that have congenital defects such as HD (hip dysplasia) or eye abnormalities, even with dogs without a pedigree. The same goes for hyperactive, nervous and shy dogs. If your Labrador does have a pedigree, then mate her with a dog that also has one. For more information, contact the breed association.

Pregnancy

It's often difficult to tell at first when a bitch is pregnant. Only after about four weeks can you feel the pups in her womb. She will now slowly get fatter and her behaviour will usually change. Her teats will swell during the last few weeks of pregnancy. The average pregnancy lasts 63 days, and costs her a lot of energy. In the beginning she is fed her normal amount of food, but her nutritional needs increase in jumps during the second half of the pregnancy. Give her approximately fifteen percent more food each week from the fifth week on. The mother-to-be needs extra energy and proteins during this phase of her pregnancy. During the last weeks you can give her a concentrated food, rich in energy, such as dry puppy food. Divide this into several small portions per day, because she can no longer deal with large portions of food. Towards the end of the pregnancy, her energy needs can easily be one-and-a-half times more than usual.

After about seven weeks the mother will start to demonstrate nesting behaviour and to look for a place to give birth to her puppies. This might be her own basket or a special whelping box. This must be ready at least a week before the birth to give the mother time to get used to it. The basket or box should preferably be in a quiet place.

The birth

The average litter is between three and nine puppies. The birth usually passes without problems. Of course, you must contact your vet immediately if you suspect a problem!

Suckling

After birth, the mother starts to produce milk. The suckling period is very demanding. During the first three to four weeks the pups rely entirely on their mother's milk. During this time she needs extra food and fluids. This can be up to three or four times the normal amount. If she's producing too little milk, you can give both mother and her young special puppy milk. Here too, divide the high quantity of food the mother needs over several smaller portions. Again, choose a concentrated, high-energy, food and give her plenty of fresh drinking water, but not cow's milk, which can cause diarrhoea.

You can give the puppies some supplemental solid food when they are three to four weeks old. There are special puppy foods available that follow on well from the mother's milk and can easily be eaten with their milk teeth. Ideally, the puppies are fully weaned at an age of six or seven weeks, i.e. they no longer drink their mother's milk. The mother's milk production gradually stops and her food needs also drop. Within a couple of weeks after weaning, the mother should again be getting the same amount of food as before the pregnancy.

Castration and sterilisation

As soon as you are sure your bitch should never bear a (new) litter, a vasectomy or sterilisation is the best solution. During sterilisation (in fact this is normal castration) the uterus is removed in an operation. The bitch no longer goes into season and can never become pregnant. The best age for a sterilisation is about eighteen months, when the bitch is more or less fully grown.

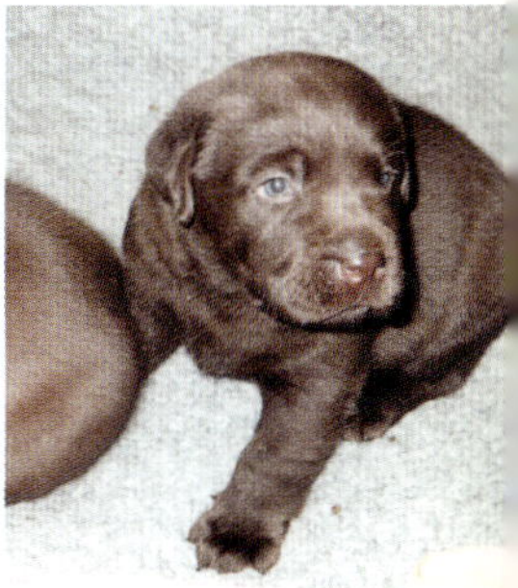

A male dog is usually only castrated for medical reasons or to correct undesirable sexual behaviour. During a castration the testicles are removed, which is a simple procedure and usually without complications. There is no special age for castration but, where possible, wait until the dog is fully grown. Vasectomy is sufficient where it's only a case of making the dog infertile. In this case the dog keeps its sexual drive but can no longer reproduce.

Sport and shows

Labradors are active dogs that won't be satisfied with the odd quiet walk. They will soon become bored and may start to display undesirable behaviour in the house.

If you want to keep a Labrador happy, you need to do things with it. An active dog needs an active master. If you regularly take part in activities with your Labrador, you will not only notice that the bond between you and your dog gets stronger, but also that your dog is quieter and more obedient. You would be amazed at the number of activities that you can participate in with a Labrador. In this chapter, we'll give you a brief overview of some of the alternatives. The breed association will be happy to help you further.

Agility

Agility is a form of dog sport where the dog accompanied by its master has to cover a set course, getting past several obstacles on the way. The trick is to get through as fast as possible with as few penalty points as possible.
Many local dog clubs organise agility competitions.

Flyball

Flyball is also a form of sport. First, the dog has to jump four hurdles and then press on a small plank. This launches a ball, which the dog has to get back to its master as fast as possible. The fastest dog wins.

Behaviour and obedience

You can pick from a whole range of obedience training courses, beginning with a puppy course. Labrador Retrievers usually enjoy this type of course. Their strong will to please means they want to perform the exercises as well as possible. After elementary obedience courses, you can train your dog for various behaviour and obedience diplomas.

Endurance test

This is primarily a European dog activity but dogs that have once learned to run alongside a bicycle usually enjoy it. And moreover, it's good for their muscle development and their body moves smoothly. Their muscles grow stronger without over-burdening their vulnerable joints. This is something that can be done along a canal towpath or along a country trail – not on a public road though. Never let your Labrador Retriever run beside the bike before it's a year old. Starting too young is bad for the development of its bones. Slowly build up the distance. Don't go out with a bike when it's too warm, don't feed your dog shortly beforehand and don't go too far. Advanced Labrador Retrievers can take part in endurance competitions. The dog has to cover a distance of twenty kilometres beside the bicycle, at a speed between fifteen and twenty kilometres per hour.

Road safety

Especially useful are road safety courses for dogs. Here, your Labrador can learn a few obedience exercises and at the end of the course can show you how safely it conducts itself in traffic.

Rescue work

The Labrador Retriever is a very capable rescue dog, but they do need thorough training first. There are groups of dog lovers that practise rescue work with their dogs as a hobby. They follow special courses and are sometimes used in disaster situations. The breed association can give you more information.

Hunting

Hunting associations often organise hunting courses, which are open to any hunting dog. A number of trainers specialise in training Labrador Retrievers. The breed associations also have special hunting examination committees.

Exhibitions and exemption shows

Visiting a dog show is a pleasant experience for both dog and master, and for some dog-lovers it is an intensive hobby. They visit countless shows every year. Others find it nice to visit an exemption show with their dog just once. It's worth making the effort to visit an exemption show where a judge's experienced eyes will inspect your Labrador Retriever and assess it for form, gait, condition and behaviour. The judge's report will teach you your dog's weak and strong points, which may help you when choosing a mate for breeding. You can also exchange experiences with other Labrador Retriever owners. Official dog shows are only open to dogs with a pedigree.

Ring training and club events

If you've never been to a dog show, you will probably be fumbling in the dark in terms of what will be expected of you and your dog. Many Labrador Retriever and general dog clubs organise so-called ring training courses for dogs going to a show for the first time. This training teaches you exactly what the judge will be looking for, and you can practise this together with your dog.

Open shows

All dog clubs organise dog shows. You must enter your dog in a certain class (in advance). These meetings are usually small and friendly and are often the first acquaintance dog and master make with a "real" judge. This is an overwhelming experience for your dog - a lot of its contemporaries and a strange man or woman who fiddles around with it and peers into its mouth. After a few times, your dog will know exactly what's expected of it and will happily go to the next club match.

Championship shows

Various championship shows take place during the course of the year with different prizes. These shows are much more strictly organised than club matches. Your dog must be registered in a certain class in advance and it will then be listed in a catalogue. On the day itself, the dog is usually kept on a bench until its turn comes up.

During the judging in the ring, it's important that you show your dog at its best. The judge examines each dog in turn. When all the dogs from that class have been judged, the best are selected and placed. After all the judging has been finished, the winners of the same sex in the different classes compete for the Challenge Certificate (3 Challenge Certificates from different judges and your Labrador Retriever will be a Champion in the UK). The best Labrador Retriever in the eyes of the judge gets this award. Finally, the winners of each sex compete for the title of Best in Show.

Of course, your dog must look very smart for the show. The judge will not be impressed if its coat is not clean or is tangled, and if its paws are dirty. Nails must be clipped and teeth free of plaque. The dog must also be free of parasites and ailments. A bitch must not be in season and a male must be in possession of both testicles. Apart from those things, judges also hate badly brought-up, anxious or nervous dogs. Get in touch with your local dog club or the breed association if you want to know more about shows.

Don't forget!

If you're planning to take your dog to a club match or in fact to any show, you need to be well prepared. Don't forget the following:

For yourself:

- Show documents if they have been sent to you
- Food and drink
- Clip for the catalogue number
- Chairs if an outdoor show

For your dog:

- Food and water bowls and food
- Dog blanket and perhaps a cushion
- Show lead
- A brush
- A benching chain and collar

Parasites

All dogs are vulnerable to various sorts of parasite. Parasites are tiny creatures that live at the expense of another animal.

They feed on blood, skin and other body substances. There are two main types. Internal parasites live within their host animal's body (tapeworm and roundworm) and external parasites live on the animal's exterior, usually in its coat (fleas and ticks), but also in its ears (ear mite).

Fleas

Fleas feed on a dog's blood. They cause not only itching and skin problems, but can also carry infections such as tapeworm. In large numbers they can cause anaemia and dogs can also become allergic to a flea's saliva, which can cause serious skin conditions. So it's important to treat dog for fleas as effectively as possible, not just on the dog itself but also in its surroundings. For treatment on the animal, there are various medicines: drops for the neck and to put in its food, flea collars, long-life sprays and flea powders. There are various sprays in pet shops that can be used to eradicate fleas in the dog's immediate surroundings. Choose a spray that kills both adult fleas and their larvae.
If your dog goes in your car, you should spray that too.
Fleas can also affect other pets, so you should treat those too.
When spraying a room, cover any aquarium or fishbowl.
If the spray reaches the water,

it can be fatal for your fish!
Your vet and pet shop have a wide range of flea treatments and can advise you on the subject.

Ticks
Ticks are small, spider-like parasites. They feed on the blood of the animal or person they've settled on. A tick looks like a tiny, grey-coloured leather bag with eight feet. When it has sucked itself full, it can easily be five to ten times its own size and is darker in colour. Dogs usually fall victim to ticks in bushes, woods or long grass. Ticks cause not only irritation by sucking blood but can also carry a number of serious diseases. This applies especially to the Mediterranean countries, which can be infested with blood parasites. In our country these diseases are fortunately less common. But Lyme disease, which can also affect humans, has reached our shores. Your vet can prescribe a special treatment if you're planning to take your dog to southern Europe. It is important to fight ticks as effectively as possible. Check your dog regularly, especially when it's been running free in woods and bushes. It can also wear an anti-tick collar.

Removing a tick is simple using a tick pincette. Grip the tick with the pincette, as close to the dog's skin as possible, and carefully pull it out. You can also grip the tick between your fingers and, using a turning movement, pull it carefully out. You must disinfect the spot where the tick was, using iodine to prevent infection. Never soak the tick in alcohol, ether or oil. In a shock reaction the tick may discharge the infected contents of its stomach into the dog's skin.

Worms
Dogs can suffer from various types of worm. The most common are tapeworm and roundworm. Tapeworm causes diarrhoea and poor condition. With a tapeworm infection you can sometimes find small pieces of the worm around the dog's anus or on its bed. In this case, the dog must be wormed. You should also check your dog for fleas, which carry the tapeworm infection.

Roundworm is a condition that reoccurs regularly. Puppies are often infected by their mother's milk. Your vet has medicines to prevent this. Roundworm causes problems (particularly in younger dogs), such as diarrhoea, loss of weight and stagnated growth. In serious cases the pup becomes thin, but with a swollen belly. It may vomit and you can then see the worms in its vomit. They are spaghetti-like tendrils.
A puppy must be treated regularly for worms with a worm treatment. Adult dogs should be treated every six months.

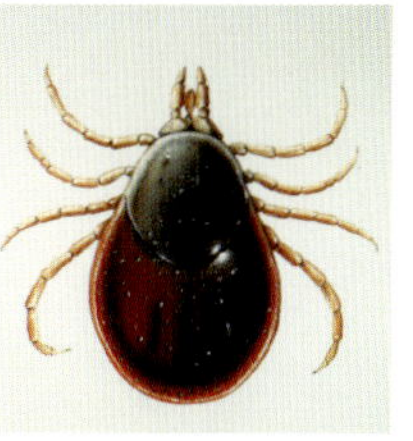

Tick

Flea

Your Labrador's health

The space in this book is too limited to go into the medical ups and downs of the Labrador Retriever. But we do want to give some brief information about ailments and disorders that affect this breed more than other dogs.

The popularity of the Labrador has had its effect on the quality of the breed. For the sake of money, a lot of breeding has taken place with unsuitable dogs, opening up more strains that are particularly vulnerable to congenital disorders.

Bone disorders

There are two forms of bone disorder to which a Labrador is particularly vulnerable:

Hip Dysplasia (HD)

Many medium to large dog breeds have problems with HD, and the Labrador is particularly vulnerable. The breed clubs are hoping to keep it under control by strict examinations of parent dogs, and make these examinations mandatory for dogs used for breeding. X-ray pictures are taken to check for a (light or serious) form of HD. Affected animals may no longer be used for breeding.

Hip dysplasia is an abnormality of the hip joint, where the hip socket doesn't properly close around the upper thigh bone. This causes inflammation and bone tumours that are very painful. Until recently, it was assumed that HD was primarily caused by genetic factors. Recent investigations, however, indicate that while genetic factors certainly play a role in terms of a dog's susceptibility to HD, external factors such as food quality and exercise appear at least equally important.

Limit the chance of HD as far as possible by giving your dog ready-made food of a good brand, and don't add any supplements! Make sure your dog doesn't get too fat. A Labrador pup should be somewhat protected from HD in its first year. Don't let it walk up and down stairs, romp too much with other dogs or chase sticks and balls too wildly. These kinds of games cause the pup to make abrupt and risky movements, which can overburden its soft joints. One important but under-estimated factor behind HD is the floor in your home. Parquet and tiled floors are much too slippery for a young dog. Regular slipping can cause complications that promote HD. If you have a smooth floor, it's advisable to lay blankets or old carpet in places the dog uses regularly. Let it spend lots of time in the garden as grass is a perfect surface to run on.

Elbow Dysplasia (ED)

Elbow dysplasia almost always manifests itself in the first year. This condition is very similar to HD, but affects the forelegs. In the worst case ED can cause lameness. An operation is then needed, which is usually successful. HD is a recognised condition, and a lot of effort is being put into eradicating it. Alas, the same does not go for ED. Although this condition is less common than HD, the Labrador is particularly vulnerable to it, so it's important to be careful that no breeding strains develop that are free of HD, but vulnerable to ED. The measures you can take to reduce the chance of ED are the same as for HD.

Eye conditions

Unfortunately, the Labrador is very vulnerable to a number of eye conditions. They need to be examined for them, even if you don't plan to breed, because most of these conditions eventually lead to blindness. These are congenital conditions, so you need to be absolutely sure of the condition of the parent animals before you buy a puppy.

Progressive Retina Atrophy (PRA)

This is a collective name for various conditions, which are a degeneration of the retina and lead to blindness. An examination is not mandatory, but the breed association urges its member to have their dogs checked for the condition, especially if they plan to breed with their dogs. Responsible breeders have their dogs examined annually. Once it's found its way into a bloodline, PRA is difficult to eradicate. In the early stages, the dog will still be able to see well in daylight until it's about five years old. But between its fifth and ninth year the dog will become totally blind.

Cataracts

Cataracts cause a clouding of the retina. The condition can occur in young animals. If only part of the retina is affected, this condition need not lead to total blindness, but unfortunately this is the consequence in most cases.

Retina Dysplasia

This is an abnormal development of the retina, which doesn't sit properly on the underlying choroid membrane. This causes wrinkles to develop in the retina. This condition arises before birth. There are three forms of RD, depending on the degree to which the retina separates, but the most serious forms are rare. The mild form causes no problems, but is becoming increasingly more common. To help eradicate this condition, it's better not to breed with dogs that suffer from even the mild form of RD.

Entropion and ectropion

These are genetic conditions affecting the eyelids. With entropion the eyelids are curled inwards, with ectropion outwards. Both cause the eyelashes to lay on the eyeball causing irritation, which leads to red, watering eyes. The eyes become infected and discharge pus, which can cause serious damage to the cornea over time, and eventually even cause blindness. Entropion and ectropion can be corrected surgically.

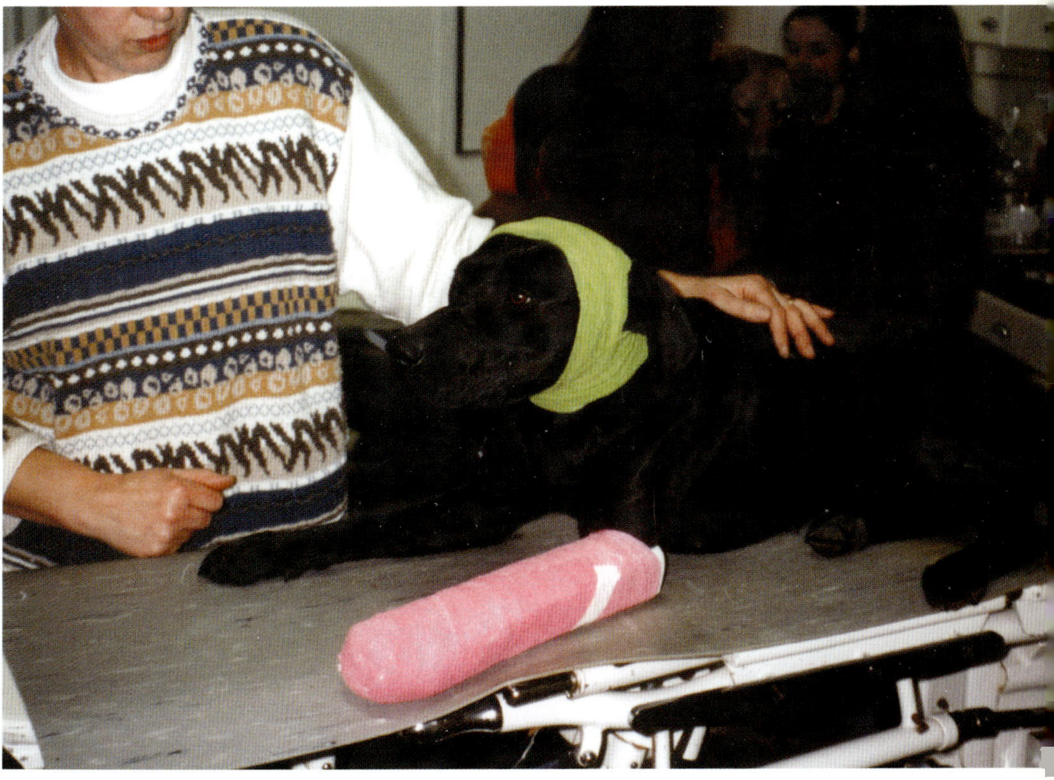

Tips

- The Labrador Retriever was originally a hunting dog; it needs a rigorous upbringing!
- Get in touch with the breed association for the address of a reliable breeder.
- Don't let your puppy run endlessly after a ball or stick.
- Don't add supplements to ready-made foods.
- Don't let your puppy up and down stairs for the first six months!
- A Labrador Retriever loves to work. Do things with it.
- Never buy a Labrador on impulse.
- Its first trip in a car is a real experience for a puppy; make it a pleasant one.
- Visit several breeders before you buy a puppy.
- Don't just fight the fleas, but the larvae too.
- Don't let your dog get too fat. Not too much food and sufficient (intelligent) exercise is the rule.
- Hard chunks and enough to chew on keep a dog's teeth healthy.
- A puppy will mean a lot of work, and sometimes a few grey hairs.
- Never buy a puppy if you haven't seen its mother!
- Good grooming is important for your dog's health.
- Always ask to see both parents' papers. The elbows and hips must have been x-rayed.
- Taking your dog with you on holiday? It's the best thing you can do.

About Pets

- The Border Collie
- The Boxer
- The Bulldog
- The Cavalier King Charles Spaniel
- The Cocker Spaniel
- The Dalmatian
- The Dobermann
- The English Springer Spaniel
- The German Shepherd
- The Golden Retriever
- The Jack Russell Terrier
- The Labrador Retriever
- The Puppy
- The Rottweiler
- The Siberian Husky
- The Shih Tzu
- The Stafforshire Bull Terrier
- The Yorkshire Terrier
- The African Grey Parrot
- The Canary
- The Budgerigar
- The Cockatiel
- The Finches
- The Lovebird
- The Parrot
- The Kitten
- The Cat
- The Siamese cats
- The Persian cat
- The Chipmunk
- The Dwarf Hamster
- The Dwarf Rabbit
- The Ferret
- The Gerbil
- The Guinea Pig
- The Hamster
- The Mouse
- The Rabbit
- The Rat
- The Goldfish
- The Tropical Fish
- The Snake
- The Tortoise

Key features of the series are:

- Most affordable books
- Packed with hands-on information
- Well written by experts
- Easy to understand language
- Full colour original photography
- 70 to 110 photos
- All one needs to know to care well for one's pet
- Trusted authors, veterinary consultants, breed and species expert authorities
- Appropriate for first time pet owners
- Interesting detailed information for pet professionals
- Title range includes books for advanced pet owners and breeders
- Includes useful addresses, veterinary data, breed standards.

about pets

A great deal of information can be found on the internet. A selection of websites with interesting details and links to other sites and pages is listed here. Sometimes pages move to another site or address. You can find more sites by using the available searchmachines.

www.thelabclub.freeserve.co.uk
The Labrador Retriever Club.

www.labrador-retriever-breeders.co.uk
On this site you can find breeders of the Labrador Retriever.

www.gaytonwood.co.uk
Breeders site with information on keeping and care of the Labrador Retriever.

www.helpalabrador.co.uk
Labrador rescue North West.

www.labrador-lifeline.co.uk
The Labrador Lifeline Trust is a Registered Charity with an operating area of Hampshire, Surrey, Berkshire, Middlesex and Lincolnshire. All money raised is used for the re-homing and welfare of the dogs.

www.alllabs.com/index.html
Online shop with Labrador products for the Labrador as well as for your home. You can also browse the "Labrador Library" for Labrador-related information on history, advice, travel etc.

www.the-kennel-club.org.uk
The Kennel Club's primary objective is to promote the general improvement of dogs in

every way. This site aims to provide you with information you may need to be a responsible pet owner and to help you keep your dog happy, safe and content.

www.k9-care.co.uk
The Self-Help site for dog owners. A beautiful website with tons of information on dogs. All you need to know about grooming, training, health care, buying a dog, travel and much more.

www.thedogscene.com/index.htm
This site is dedicated to pedigree dogs in the United Kingdom. Dog breeds, articles, shopping mall are a number of the issues you can find on this website.

www.pet-insurance-uk.me.uk
Find low cost pet insurance via this UK pet insurance directory.

www.pethealthcare.co.uk
At PEThealthcare.co.uk they believe that a healthy pet is a happy pet.
Which is why they've brought together leading experts to create a comprehensive online source of pet care information.

www.waltham.com
Waltham is a firm specialized in pet care and nutrition. On this website you can find more information on pet care, training and more.

www.onlinepetcare.co.uk
www.onlinepetcare.co.uk was launched in 2001 and contains information about and links to businesses and charities in the Midlands area involved in the care and purchasing of domestic animals.

http://champdogs.co.uk
Search the champ dogs database for kennels, stud dogs and litters.

www.mypetstop.com
An international, multilingual website with information on keeping, breeding, behaviour, health related issues and much more.

http://dogtraining.co.uk
Your central resource for dog-training, boarding kennels & vets in the UK.

www.aboutpets.info
The website of the publisher of the About Pets book series. An overview of the titles, availability in which languages and where in the world the books are sold.

Breed Associations

Becoming a member of a breeder club can be very useful for good advice and interesting activities. Contact the Kennel Club in case addresses or telephonenumbers have changed.

Kennelclubs in Great Britain

The Kennel Club
1 Clarges Street
London UK
WIJ 8AB
Tel: 0870 606 6750
Fax: 020 7518 1058
www.the-kennelclub.org.uk

Scottish Kennel Club
Eskmills Park
Station Road
Musselborough EH21 7PQ
Tel: 0131 6653920
Fax: 01316536937
Email: info@scottishkennelclub.org
www.scottishkennelclub.org

The Irish Kennel Club Ltd.
Fottrell house,
Harold's
Cross Bridge,
Dublin 6W
Ireland
Tel: (01) 4533300 - 4532309 - 4532310.
Fax: (01) 4533237
Email: ikenclub@indigo.ie
www.ikc.i.e

Cotswold & Wyevern Labrador Club
Sec. Mr Collins
Tel: 01452 780635

East Anglian Labrador Retriever Club
Sec. Mrs J Cole
Tel: 01354680375

Kent Surrey & Sussex Labrador Retriever Club
Sec. Mrs Saunderson
Tel: 01306 881231

Labrador Club of Scotland
Sec. Mrs A M Pollock
Tel: 01563 820270

Labrador Retriever Club
Sec. Mrs S M B Walton
Tel: 01279 655937

Labrador Retriever Club of Northern Ireland
Sec. Mrs C F Doherty
Tel: 01846 639264

Labrador Retriever of Wales
Sec. Mrs J Povall
Tel: 01633 422638

Midland Counties Labrador Retriever Club
Sec. Mrs J Allen
Tel: 01733 222649

North West Labrador Retriever
Sec. Mrs S M Saunt
Tel: 01942 212280

Northumberland & Durham Labrador Retriever
Sec. Mr p a smith
Tel: 01642 292965

Three Ridings Labrador club
Sec. Mrs P Gill
Tel: 01943 467926

West of England Labrador Retriever Club
Sec. Mr G P Fox
Tel: 01566 785121

Yellow Labrador Club
Sec. Mrs Wiles
Tel: 01895 823227

Group:	Gundogs	
First standard:	1903 (England)	
Breed association founded:	1916 (England)	
Origin:	Newfoundland (Canada)	
Original tasks:	Helping to bring in fish catches / hunting dog	
Shoulder height	Dog:	55.5-57 cm
	Bitch:	54-56 cm
Weight	Dog:	27-34 kg
	Bitch:	25-32 kg
Average life expectancy:	12 years